Original title:

Bonds that Heal

Author: Lan Donne

ISBN HARDBACK: 978-9916-89-136-0

ISBN PAPERBACK: 978-9916-89-137-7

ISBN EBOOK: 978-9916-89-138-4

The Sweetness of Shared Grief

In silence we sit, side by side,
Hearts heavy, but stars still hide.
A tear falls, like a rain of pain,
Yet in this sorrow, there's comfort gained.

Memories linger, softly they breathe,
Whispers of love in memories weave.
Together we honor what once was bright,
In the darkness, we find our light.

Pillars of Support

Strong hands uplift, never let go,
In tough times, they steadily flow.
Each heartbeat whispers, 'You're not alone,'
Together we build, a sturdy home.

Through storms we stand, unwavering and true,
In laughter and tears, we carry through.
A bond unshakable, like roots of a tree,
In this fortress of trust, we are free.

The Fire of Connection

A spark ignites in the quiet of night,
Two souls entwined, the world feels right.
With every glance, a flame takes flight,
In warmth we dance, lost in the light.

Conversations flow, like rivers of gold,
Stories shared, as mysteries unfold.
With every heartbeat, passion grows,
In the fire of love, true connection glows.

Azure Skies of Togetherness

Under vast skies, with hope held high,
Dreams painted bright, like clouds passing by.
Hand in hand, through laughter we roam,
In the warm sun, we've found our home.

Together we chase all the stars above,
In every moment, we cherish love.
With open hearts and eyes that see,
In azure skies, you're here with me.

Tethered in Trust

In shadows cast by doubt,
We find strength in the ties,
Whispers weave through the night,
Together, we rise.

Hearts bound by gentle care,
Like roots of the old trees,
In storms, we stand our ground,
With love as our breeze.

Trust is the thread we hold,
Worn and frayed but still strong,
Through trials, it does not break,
It carries us along.

Each secret, softly shared,
A lantern in our chest,
We nurture what is real,
In each, we find our rest.

So let the world unfold,
With all its twists and turns,
In trust, we build our home,
Where love forever burns.

Light After the Storm

The clouds have rolled away,
Revealing skies of blue,
With every drop that fell,
The earth drinks in the hue.

Beneath the silver rain,
The blooms lift up their heads,
Their colors shine anew,
Where once were tears and reds.

A gentle breeze now plays,
Through trees that sway and dance,
It carries forth the sound,
Of nature's sweet romance.

We gather in the warmth,
Of sun's embracing glow,
Rebirth within the heart,
Through paths we long to go.

The storm has shaped our souls,
Like pebbles shaped by time,
In light, we find our strength,
Our spirits in their prime.

Notes of Grace

In every quiet moment,
A melody persists,
A whisper of the heart,
In soft, unbroken lists.

The dusk wraps tones of peace,
Where shadows dance and fold,
Each note an embrace given,
A story to be told.

Through trials and the tears,
We find a soothing sound,
For grace is in the chaos,
In silence, it is found.

With every step we take,
A harmony unfolds,
In laughter shared with friends,
And warmth when night is cold.

So let our lives compose,
A symphony so wide,
With notes of grace and love,
Forever as our guide.

Wounds and Wings

The scars that mark our skin,
Tell tales of fights within,
With every crack and crease,
A deeper strength begins.

We rise from pain and loss,
Like birds against the tide,
Each wound a feathered part,
In which our hope can glide.

The broken moments teach,
Resilience found in grief,
For in our darkest nights,
We gather light's belief.

With wings stretched ever wide,
We soar beyond the strain,
The past may weigh us down,
Yet still, we dance through pain.

So let us fly, my dear,
With wounds that shape our song,
For in our scars we stitch,
A life where we belong.

Skylines of Hope

Beneath the towering spires,
Dreams touch the endless skies.
In every vibrant color,
A promise slowly flies.

The sun begins to rise,
Casting warmth on hearts anew.
Each glance at distant heights,
Whispers, 'You can break through.'

In the bustling city scene,
Hope dances hand in hand.
With every step we take,
Together we will stand.

The clouds may sometimes gather,
Cast shadows on our way.
Yet still we strive for clarity,
And brighter, better days.

From concrete peaks to valleys,
We chase the gleaming light.
In the skylines of our dreams,
Hope always takes its flight.

Embracing Fragility

Like petals in the breeze,
We sway with every breath.
In the gentle moments,
We find our strength in death.

A teardrop tells a story,
Of beauty in the pain.
With every crack and fracture,
New life will form again.

We learn to hold each other,
In silence and in grace.
In the softest whispers,
We find our rightful place.

Together, we are fragile,
Yet stronger than we seem.
In the delicate spaces,
We weave our quiet dream.

Embracing all our layers,
The tender and the bold.
In the arms of fragility,
Our hearts will never fold.

Lighthouses in the Storm

Amidst the raging waters,
A beacon stands so bright.
Through chaos and the tempest,
It guides us to the light.

With every crashing wave,
We search for solid ground.
In the fierce wind's howl,
Our hope is still unbound.

The storm can shake our courage,
Yet we will not despair.
For lighthouses of kindness,
Are scattered everywhere.

We gather strength from love,
As we weather the night.
With each other's presence,
We turn the dark to light.

When tides seem never-ending,
And skies refuse to clear,
We are the lighthouses,
Shining bright, always near.

A Quilt of Togetherness

Stitched with threads of laughter,
Each patch a story told.
In warmth of shared embraces,
We find a love to hold.

The colors interwoven,
In patterns rich and bright.
Together we create,
A tapestry of light.

Our hearts a cozy fabric,
Embroidered with our dreams.
In every seam united,
Our bond forever gleams.

Through storms and sunny days,
We gather 'round to share.
The beauty in our quilt,
Is woven with such care.

In the softness of our love,
We find a home at last.
A quilt of togetherness,
Where future meets the past.

Echoes of Understanding

In the silence of the night,
Whispers weave through the air.
Hearts beat in shared light,
Finding solace in despair.

Through shadows of our past,
We search for common ground.
In every question cast,
Answers in love are found.

Time reveals our truths,
In laughter, in our tears.
Learning from the youth,
Compassion calms our fears.

Echoes linger long,
A melody of grace.
In every heart, a song,
A gentle, warm embrace.

When we dare to see,
Beyond the veil of pain,
In unity, we're free,
Echoes will remain.

Tapestry of Kindred Souls

Threads of fate interlace,
Binding us ever tight.
In each other, we trace,
The beauty of shared light.

Colors blend, hearts unfold,
Stories stitched with care.
In warmth, our truths are told,
A bond beyond compare.

Moments woven in time,
Frayed edges hold the strength.
In rhythm and in rhyme,
We find our shared length.

With every tear we mend,
The fabric grows so rich,
In the warmth of a friend,
Life's stitches never hitch.

Hand in hand, we weave fate,
Knots that never may break.
In the love we create,
A tapestry we make.

Roots of Redemption

In the soil of our dreams,
Seeds of hope take their place.
With sunlight, life redeems,
Nurtured by love's embrace.

Through struggles, we will grow,
Finding strength in the fight.
In darkness, we will know,
That truth reveals the light.

As branches stretch so wide,
We'll rise above the storm.
In unity, we bide,
Together, we are warm.

The scars of yesterday,
A testament of grace.
In every step we sway,
We find our sacred space.

When we reach toward the sky,
Roots hold firm in the ground.
In our hearts, we'll fly,
Redemption is our sound.

Fragile Strength

In the hush of the dawn,
Soft whispers break the night.
Where the brave have drawn,
Lines of courage in fight.

Beneath the surface, still,
A power grows within.
In the shadows, we will,
Face the battles we've been.

With each falling tear,
We rise to meet the day.
In moments, crystal clear,
We find the strength to stay.

Though the winds may howl,
And the storms may rage hard,
In the voices that prowl,
Hope is the steady guard.

In the heart's quiet plea,
Fragility stands tall.
For in our unity,
Strength is the greatest call.

Threads of Serenity

In the quiet hush of dawn,
Whispers of peace are drawn.
Gentle breezes caress the trees,
While hearts find their ease.

Beneath the arching skies,
Hope begins to rise.
The world is still and bright,
Wrapped in soft, golden light.

Moments weave like delicate lace,
Filling every space.
Each thread a quiet sigh,
As time glides gently by.

In stillness, we discover
The bonds that softly hover.
Reaching, knitting day by day,
Threads of serenity sway.

With every breath we take,
Restoring all that breaks.
A tapestry of bliss,
Finding joy in each kiss.

The Light Beneath

In shadows deep, there's a spark,
A flicker bright in the dark.
With courage, we take a stand,
Finding strength, hand in hand.

Through trials and the night,
We chase after the light.
With each step, fear will cease,
Unafraid, we find peace.

In laughter's joyful sound,
Hope and love abound.
Together we will rise,
Reaching towards the skies.

The light that warms the soul,
Makes the broken whole.
In kindness, we believe,
It's in giving that we receive.

So hold on to dreams that gleam,
Let them flow like a stream.
We'll walk this path with faith,
Illuminated by grace.

Healing Through Laughter

In moments shared, joy appears,
Wiping away all fears.
Laughter dances in the air,
Binding hearts with tender care.

With every giggle, a lift,
Healing's warm and precious gift.
A spark ignites, bright and clear,
Turning sorrow into cheer.

In the stories that we tell,
We weave a magic spell.
Through the cracks we find the light,
In shadows banished by delight.

With friends around, we mend,
The broken hearts will blend.
Through laughter, we redefine,
The power of the divine.

So let the laughter ring,
As our spirits take to wing.
In every joyous refrain,
Together we shall rise again.

Heartstrings Entwined

Two souls meet in a glance,
In the depths, there's a chance.
Through laughter and whispers soft,
Together, we float aloft.

In rhythms shared, we sway,
Finding words that play.
With every heartbeat's race,
Time unravels with grace.

The melodies of our sighs,
Carry dreams to the skies.
Entwined in the night's embrace,
Fate leaves a gentle trace.

Through storms that may arise,
We'll brave them, you and I.
With love's unbreakable thread,
In harmony, we'll tread.

For every path we roam,
In your heart, I find home.
Together, we shall sing,
To the joys that love can bring.

A Tapestry of Tenderness

In soft whispers, love is sewn,
Each thread a story, gently grown.
Colors blend in harmony,
A quilt of hearts, our tapestry.

Through trials faced, we stand as one,
With every tear, more strength is spun.
Together we will weave our tale,
In every storm, we will not fail.

In each embrace, warm fabric feels,
Every heartbeat, softness heals.
With threads of kindness, we unite,
A tapestry that holds us tight.

As seasons change, so may we grow,
New patterns formed, yet love will flow.
In every stitch, a bond profound,
A tapestry where peace is found.

So let us weave with steady hands,
Creating beauty where love stands.
In colors bold and shadows deep,
A tapestry of dreams we keep.

Sanctuary in Unity

In quiet peace, we gather near,
With open hearts, we hold what's dear.
The world outside may roar and quake,
But in this place, all fears we'll shake.

A circle drawn with trust and care,
Each voice a song, a gentle prayer.
Together we can face the night,
In unity, we find our light.

Through laughter shared and tears released,
Our sanctuary, where love increased.
In every hug, a fierce embrace,
We build a home, a sacred space.

No judgment here, just warmth and grace,
A haven where we find our place.
In moments quiet, in joy's bright hue,
We stand as one, our bond is true.

So let our hearts forever beat,
In rhythms shared, we feel complete.
A sanctuary where we belong,
In unity, we share our song.

The Glow of Reassurance

In shadows deep, a light will shine,
With gentle flames, hearts will align.
The glow of hope, it warms the night,
A beacon bold, a guiding light.

With every whisper, fears subside,
In moments shared, we take the ride.
Through storms of doubt, we won't despair,
Together wrapped in tender care.

In laughter bright, we find our way,
With every step, come what may.
The glow persists, through thick and thin,
In love's embrace, we always win.

No need for words, just presence near,
In silence, too, we hold what's dear.
The glow of trust lights up the dark,
In every heart, we find our spark.

So let us cherish, hold it dear,
The glow of reassurance, loud and clear.
For in this warmth, we will remain,
Together, always, through joy and pain.

Tides of Companionship

With every wave, we rise and fall,
In oceans deep, we hear the call.
Together we will navigate,
Through calm and storm, we share our fate.

The tides may shift, the currents change,
Yet hand in hand, we'll rearrange.
In every swell, in every sigh,
We find our strength, we learn to fly.

In sandy shores, our laughter rings,
Together, face the joys life brings.
Through whispers soft and shouts of glee,
Companionship, our symphony.

As twilight dawns and stars arise,
We share our dreams beneath the skies.
In every tide that pulls us close,
Together still, we love the most.

So here we stand, through time and space,
In salty air, we find our grace.
With every turn of tide we see,
Companionship, our legacy.

The Power of Shared Silence

In quiet moments, hearts align,
Words unspoken, pure and fine.
Two souls dwell in tranquil light,
A bond that glimmers, soft and bright.

The stillness speaks what words can't say,
In silence, love finds its way.
Connection deep in every breath,
A whispered promise, life and death.

Time stretches long, yet feels so brief,
In shared silence, find relief.
The world outside fades far away,
In this space, we choose to stay.

Eyes meet gently, a knowing glance,
In silence lies a sacred dance.
The echoes of the heart resound,
In every pause, true peace is found.

So let us cherish moments shared,
In silent vows, our hearts declared.
For here in stillness, love ignites,
In every hush, our dreams take flight.

From Ashes to Embrace

From ashes grey, new life will rise,
Through shattered dreams, the spirit flies.
Each ember warms the coldest night,
In dying flames, we find the light.

With every tear, a seed is sown,
From pain's embrace, the heart has grown.
The past may burn, but hope remains,
In every loss, new strength now gains.

We rise like phoenix, fierce and bold,
Transforming hurt into pure gold.
In fire's heart, we find our grace,
From scorched earth blooms a warm embrace.

The journey long, the path unclear,
Yet through the trials, love draws near.
With open arms, we face the storms,
From ashes, life, in myriad forms.

So hold my hand, let's take this flight,
Out of the dark, into the light.
From ashes scattered, we create,
A world where love can resonate.

Unseen Threads

Invisible strands that bind us tight,
Across the miles, a shared delight.
In dreams we weave, in whispers flow,
The unseen ties that gently grow.

With every thought, we bridge the space,
In perfect harmony, we find our place.
Connected souls, though far apart,
These threads of love unite the heart.

A gentle touch, though miles between,
In silent echoes, what might have been.
The fabric rich with colors bright,
A tapestry of purest light.

Through time and space, these threads won't fray,
In every dawn, a brand new day.
In laughter shared, in tears we shed,
The woven paths where hearts are led.

So let us cherish every thread,
For in this weave, love's story spreads.
With unseen ties, we rise and shine,
In every heart, our souls entwine.

Heartstrings Entwined

Two hearts that beat in gentle sync,
With every glance, they seem to think.
In every note, a song is played,
With love's embrace, we are remade.

Through whispered dreams in the night,
Our heartstrings pull, a force of light.
In harmony, we find our way,
Together bright, we'll face the day.

The world may shift, the ground may part,
Yet here we stand, and never part.
With every challenge, we will rise,
In love's sweet dance, we find the ties.

Like vines that twist and intertwine,
Our spirits soar; our souls align.
In every breath, we draw so close,
In heartstrings bound, we love the most.

So let the music play anew,
With every note, I choose you too.
In every moment, hand in hand,
Together strong, together stand.

Unraveled to Rebuild

Threads of thought come undone,
Scattered dreams lost in the run.
Yet in silence, wisdom grows,
From the chaos, strength arose.

Torn pieces search for their place,
In the void, we find our grace.
Like a puzzle, we reframe,
Building paths to reignite flame.

In the dark, a spark ignites,
New foundations in moonlight.
With each breath, we claim the night,
Unraveled hearts find the light.

Hope whispers through the dismay,
Guiding us to a new way.
From the ashes, we will rise,
In unity, we'll claim the skies.

Together, mending the seams,
Weave the fabric of our dreams.
With each stitch, we redefine,
Unraveled hearts, now intertwined.

The Garden of Reconnection

In a garden where we meet,
Old roots intertwine at our feet.
Flowers bloom, colors blend,
Nature teaches how to mend.

Soft breezes share their tales,
Of lost journeys and new trails.
Buds of hope begin to sprout,
In this space, we find the route.

Sunlight dances on our skin,
As warm laughter pulls us in.
Every moment, gently sown,
In this garden, we have grown.

Birdsong weaves through the air,
Reminding us that love is rare.
With open hearts, we can see,
Together, we are wild and free.

As we tend to fragile blooms,
We nurture joy that brightly looms.
In reconnection, we find peace,
In the garden, our hearts release.

Cadence of Care

In soft whispers, kindness flows,
Gentle presence, warmth that shows.
Every gesture, small and bright,
Creates a rhythm, feels so right.

Like a heartbeat in the night,
Care surrounds, holding us tight.
In the dance of give and take,
With each step, new paths we make.

Through the storms, we stand as one,
Sharing burdens 'til they're done.
In the cadence, love prevails,
In each heartbeat, hope unveils.

Over mountains, through the pain,
Together, sunshine through the rain.
With compassion, we will thrive,
In the cadence, we are alive.

Every echo of our song,
Reminds us where we all belong.
With every note, we find our way,
In the cadence, love will stay.

Harmonies of Healing

In the silence, we hear a tune,
Whispers soft as a fading moon.
Healing starts in gentle waves,
Lifting us from hidden caves.

Voices blend in sweet surround,
Melodies lost, now found.
With each note, we mend the past,
In the harmony, love will last.

Strings of hearts begin to play,
Notes of joy chase tears away.
In shared harmonies, we find,
Unity of body and mind.

As the music swells and thrives,
Healing echoes, love survives.
Together, we create our song,
In these harmonies, we belong.

With every breath, we heal anew,
Songs of hope, both old and true.
In this place, we reclaim the feel,
In harmonies, together, we heal.

Ties of Resilience

In storms we find our strength,
Roots entwined beneath the ground.
With every challenge we face,
Together, we stand our ground.

The winds may howl and shake the trees,
Yet our bond will not break.
Through trials, we weave our tales,
In unity, we awake.

Each setback is a chance to grow,
To fortify our spirit's might.
Through shadows cast, we will glow,
Illuminated by shared light.

When doubts creep in and fears arise,
We lift each other high.
In the embrace of trust, we rise,
Reaching for the sky.

With love as our guiding thread,
We stitch our dreams anew.
In resilience, we are led,
A tapestry of truth.

The Salve of Togetherness

In laughter shared and whispered dreams,
We find the balm for weary souls.
A gentle touch in silent screams,
Together, we feel whole.

With every joy and every tear,
A circle forms, unbreakable.
In moments spent, we draw near,
Creating something beautiful.

Through trials faced, with hearts that bleed,
We nurse each other's pain.
In unity, we plant a seed,
Of hope that will remain.

In shared burdens, lighter roads,
We carry each other's weight.
With every step, love slowly loads,
A bond we cultivate.

Hand in hand, we walk through fire,
Emerging strong, side by side.
In this bond, our hearts aspire,
To flourish, undenied.

Mending Hearts in Harmony

With gentle hands, we stitch the seams,
Of lives once torn apart.
We gather fragments, share our dreams,
Mending every heart.

In fragile whispers, truths unfold,
Creating melody anew.
As stories shared, our strength will fold,
In colors vibrant and true.

Through soothing words and tender care,
We weave our hopes with grace.
In every loss, we find repair,
Together, we embrace.

In unity, our voices swell,
A chorus strong and clear.
As one, we rise, together dwell,
In harmony, we steer.

With every beat, we heal the scars,
And honor what we've learned.
Together, we will reach for stars,
With love, our hearts have burned.

Affinity's Embrace

In gentle moments, eyes collide,
A spark ignites the air.
In quiet tones, we confide,
Our souls laid bare.

With every laugh that lights the room,
Connection's thread is spun.
In shared silences, we bloom,
Two hearts beat as one.

Through pathways winding, hand in hand,
We chase the setting sun.
In togetherness, we understand,
Our journey's just begun.

When shadows cast their fleeting hue,
Our bond will guide the way.
In all we are, and all we do,
Affinity will stay.

With open hearts and minds set free,
We embrace the ebb and flow.
In unity, we find the key,
To love and let it grow.

Echoes of Understanding

In silence, we find hidden truths,
Words unspoken weave their way,
Hearts listening, gentle and warm,
In shared moments, we learn to stay.

Fleeting shadows dance in the night,
Thoughts like whispers softly flow,
Bound by empathy's gentle light,
We bridge the gaps, allow love to grow.

Each glance exchanged holds a story,
A journey through laughter and pain,
In the stillness, we find our glory,
Drawing strength from joy and rain.

Through the echoes of time we wander,
Sharing burdens, lifting the load,
In every heartbeat, we ponder,
Together, we walk this shared road.

In twilight, our spirits entwine,
United in hope, we shall find,
A garden of dreams in decline,
Together, our souls are aligned.

The Warmth of Sympathetic Hearts

In the glow of a soft, amber light,
Hands reach out, eager to touch,
A spark ignites in the quiet night,
Revealing the depth of our hearts' clutch.

Each smile brings comfort, each laugh a balm,
In the warmth, our fears disband,
A gentle embrace, so sweet, so calm,
We weave a tapestry hand in hand.

Through the storms, we find our peace,
In understanding, we rise above,
Healing begins, all troubles cease,
In the sanctuary of our love.

Our words are soft, like a flowing stream,
They carry the promise of what can be,
Together, we foster the brightest dream,
In the cocoon of shared symphony.

As shadows fade into night's embrace,
We stand as one against the cold,
With every heartbeat, we find our place,
In the warmth of love's gentle hold.

Rewoven Souls

In the loom of life, threads intertwine,
Stories woven with care and grace,
Colors blend, as destinies align,
Each soul a pattern, a warm embrace.

Tales of laughter, threads of sorrow,
Together we craft a vibrant quilt,
Each day brings hope for tomorrow,
With love as the fabric, our world is built.

In every stitch, a promise made,
We mend the broken, heal the pain,
Through joy and grief, we aren't afraid,
For in unity, our strength remains.

As time unravels the years we trace,
In the patterns, our essence flows,
Each moment cherished, no time to waste,
Our rewoven souls in beauty glow.

At dusk, we gather under fading light,
With threads that bind us, strong and true,
In every heartbeat, pure delight,
Together, we paint a vivid view.

Kindred Spirits at Twilight

Beneath the stars, we come alive,
In whispered secrets shared so low,
Two kindred souls, our spirits thrive,
As twilight casts its gentle glow.

In the hush, our laughter rings clear,
A melody carried on the breeze,
With every moment, we draw near,
In harmony, we find our ease.

Through winding paths of moonlit dreams,
We wander, hand in hand, side by side,
In nature's silence, our heart redeems,
Together, we embrace the tide.

Each shadow stretching, dancing wide,
We forge a bond that cannot break,
In the twilight, our hearts confide,
A love so deep, no path forsake.

As stars emerge and daylight fades,
We celebrate the night's embrace,
In the glow of dreams, our hope cascades,
Two kindred spirits, a sacred space.

Foundations of Affection

In quiet corners, love is sown,
Where gentle whispers softly thrive.
Each tender moment, seeds are grown,
In the heart's garden, love's alive.

Through shared laughter, bonds unite,
Embracing flaws we come to see.
Together, facing day and night,
In every breath, we feel the free.

With open arms, we weave our fate,
In the warmth of trust, we stand tall.
In simple gestures, we create,
A home of love, where hearts won't fall.

Through storms and calm, we will endure,
With roots so deep, we will not break.
In every heartbeat, love is pure,
A sturdy bond that none can shake.

As sun sets low, our shadows blend,
In twilight's glow, our hearts align.
Forevermore, we won't pretend,
Foundations strong, forever shine.

The Beauty of Mutual Care

In kindness shared, the world transforms,
Each small act sends ripples wide.
Together we weather the fiercest storms,
With hearts that beat, side by side.

From gentle words to a helping hand,
Compassion dances in our eyes.
In every moment, we understand,
True beauty within, it never lies.

A warm embrace, a listening ear,
In silence loud, we hold the space.
With open hearts, we draw near,
In tender love, we find our grace.

Through laughter shared, and tears we shed,
In vulnerability, we find strength.
Each story told, each wound we've bled,
We stitch together, our love's length.

With every heartbeat, we declare,
A promise forged in life's embrace.
Together, we nurture and repair,
In mutual care, we find our place.

Healing Hands, Open Hearts

With every touch, the world can change,
A simple gesture, love bestowed.
In healing hands, hearts re-arrange,
As hope's bright light begins to glow.

Through trials faced and burdens shared,
We rise together, strong and free.
In moments when we felt impaired,
Your presence brings tranquility.

With open hearts, we break the walls,
Embracing each soul as it comes.
In laughter's echo, stillness calls,
A symphony, where love hums.

Through gentle hugs and soothing words,
The scars that mark can fade away.
Together, we can mend the birds,
And help the weary find their way.

In shadows cast, the light breaks through,
With every heartbeat, we align.
Healing hands and whispers true,
In open hearts, love's pure design.

The Mosaic of Compassion

In pieces gathered from our past,
With colors bright, we form the whole.
In every story, shadows cast,
We find in pain, the healer's role.

With kindness woven through the cracks,
A tapestry of strength we weave.
In giving hope, we find the tracks,
Of paths where all can dare believe.

Each shard a lesson from the heart,
In empathy, we learn to stand.
Through every tear, a brand new start,
Together we, as one, expand.

No longer bound by judgment's chain,
We honor every voice we hear.
In unity, we break the pain,
Transforming doubt into a cheer.

With every moment's gentle squeeze,
Compassion blooms in vibrant hue.
A mosaic formed, our souls at ease,
In every heartbeat, love shines through.

The Magic of Shared Moments

In laughter's light, we find our way,
Together, we weave the colors of day.
In whispered dreams, our spirits dance,
Moments shared, a timeless romance.

Through starlit skies, our hearts ignite,
Every shared glance, a spark so bright.
In silence, we craft a language sweet,
Every heartbeat an echo, a rhythmic beat.

With hands entwined, we face the unknown,
In the tapestry of life, our love has grown.
Through every storm, we stand so tall,
Shared moments, the treasures that bind us all.

In fleeting hours, like grains of sand,
We hold the magic in our hands.
Every smile, a memory to keep,
In the gentle night, our promises seep.

Unforgettable echoes of joy and pain,
In both sunshine and in the rain.
Together we journey, through thick and thin,
Forever the magic, where we begin.

Healing in the Afterglow

After the storm, a quiet sigh,
In tender light, we learn to fly.
With every tear, a new dawn breaks,
In the stillness, our spirit wakes.

Wounds once raw begin to mend,
In the shadows, we find a friend.
With gentle whispers on the breeze,
Hope emerges, bringing us ease.

We gather light from darkened days,
In healing, there are countless ways.
Each scar tells stories, brave and true,
In the afterglow, we find our due.

Through whispered prayers and starry nights,
We rise anew, embracing the heights.
With hearts ignited, we walk the line,
In the afterglow, our souls align.

So let the past fall where it may,
In every moment, let love stay.
With open arms, we bid adieu,
To pain and sorrow, welcome what's new.

Embraces that Mend

In the warmth of a hug, we find our home,
Two souls entwined, no longer alone.
With every squeeze, the world seems right,
In such embraces, we take flight.

Through trials faced, we stand as one,
In silent strength, the healing's begun.
With gentle hands, we weave the thread,
Embraces, the language that's often said.

Each touch, a promise, soft and true,
In the heart's rhythm, I find you.
In moments shared, we learn to heal,
Through every embrace, our wounds conceal.

In laughter's echo or bitter tears,
In every embrace, we face our fears.
Together we mend, with grace bestowed,
In the sacred space, our love has flowed.

So let the world spin, let it sway,
In each embrace, we'll find our way.
With open hearts, together we'll blend,
In every moment, the love we send.

Harmony in the Heartache

In shadows cast by love's sweet game,
We find our truth, not just the blame.
With heavy hearts, we learn to sing,
In harmony wrapped, our spirits cling.

Through tears we flow, like rivers wide,
In heartache's grip, we must abide.
Yet, through the storm, a melody grows,
In every note, our healing shows.

With every loss, there's always gain,
In darkened skies, we seek the rain.
From shattered dreams, new visions rise,
In unity found, there lies the prize.

We walk this path, both sad and bright,
With every step, we find our light.
In heartache's whisper, we learn to play,
In harmony's embrace, we'll find our way.

For love is music, soft and wide,
It teaches us how to abide.
In every heartache, a lesson stays,
In harmony's tune, life sways.

Awakened Hearts

In quiet dawn, the whispers rise,
Hearts unbound, beneath the skies.
With every breath, a spark ignites,
Awoken souls, chasing the lights.

A gentle sway, the world in bloom,
Together we dispel the gloom.
Each glance a promise, tender and true,
Awakened hearts, me and you.

Embrace the warmth, the love we share,
In silent moments, beyond all care.
With every heartbeat, we grow strong,
To sing together, our sacred song.

Through open fields, we dare to roam,
In every step, we find our home.
Awakened hearts, forever free,
In this dance of you and me.

Time may wander, but love will stay,
Guiding our dreams, lighting the way.
Awakened hearts, we'll make our mark,
Together blazing through the dark.

Nurtured Through Time

In the garden where memories grow,
Seeds of kindness, gentle and slow.
Nurtured by love, we learn and thrive,
In the embrace of a life alive.

Through storms and sun, we find our way,
Holding on tight, come what may.
With hands entwined, we face the years,
Nurtured through laughter, healed through tears.

Stories shared and lessons learned,
In the heart's hearth, our passion burned.
Each chapter penned, a tale divine,
Together shining, a love benign.

Tides may rise, yet we stand firm,
In the dance of life, we twist and turn.
Nurtured through time, our roots grow deep,
In the sacred promise that we keep.

As seasons change, the years unfold,
A tapestry of memories bold.
In every heartbeat, our essence blends,
Nurtured through time, our love transcends.

Crossroads of Compassion

At the crossroads where choices lay,
Compassion lights the hidden way.
With gentle hearts, we lend a hand,
In the silence, we understand.

Paths intertwine, a dance so fine,
In moments shared, hearts realign.
A tender gaze, an open ear,
Crossroads of compassion, drawing near.

With every step, we choose to care,
In times of joy, in times of despair.
Together we rise, united, strong,
Crossroads of compassion, where we belong.

Through trials faced, our spirits soar,
In giving love, we find much more.
A lifeline cast where shadows fall,
Together we rise, together stand tall.

In this embrace, we weave our fate,
In kindness shared, we elevate.
Crossroads of compassion, forever bright,
Guiding us home to the light.

Seasons of Renewal

In springtime's grace, the blooms appear,
Whispers of hope, a song sincere.
With every petal, a promise made,
Seasons of renewal, never fade.

Summer's warmth, the laughter rings,
In golden light, the joy it brings.
With open hearts, we share our days,
Seasons of renewal, in endless ways.

As autumn winds, the colors change,
Embracing all, both small and strange.
A dance of leaves, the air so clear,
Seasons of renewal, drawing near.

In winter's chill, we find the peace,
In quiet moments, our fears release.
Together we gather, stories flow,
Seasons of renewal, love will grow.

Through every cycle, we learn and bend,
Life's gentle rhythm, our cherished friend.
Seasons of renewal, forever sing,
In nature's arms, new joys we bring.

Echoes of Kindness

In the quiet whispers of the night,
Kindness dances, soft and bright.
A gesture small, a smile wide,
Spreading warmth like the rising tide.

Each heart beats in a gentle tune,
A melody under the silver moon.
Echoes linger, hearts set free,
In a world where love should be.

Gentle touches, hands entwined,
In moments that are undefined.
A shared laugh upon the street,
Kindness travels, never discreet.

So let us nurture each kind deed,
Plant the love, and see it breed.
For in the echoes, we'll find our way,
A brighter path with each new day.

In every heart, a seed is sown,
With kindness, we are never alone.
Hear the echoes that softly call,
Together, we can rise or fall.

The Gentle Tug of Affection

In the morning light, your eyes gleam,
A gentle tug, an unspoken dream.
Soft as whispers that fill the air,
With every glance, I'm stripped bare.

Your laughter dances on the breeze,
A melody that brings me peace.
Wrapped in warmth, I feel the pull,
In your embrace, I'm truly full.

When shadows loom and worries grow,
The gentle tug pulls me, you know.
In the stillness, our hearts collide,
An unseen force that won't subside.

Every moment's a cherished gift,
In your presence, my spirits lift.
Through life's storms, we find our way,
With the tug of love in bright array.

So hold me close, let worries fade,
In the simplicity of this cascade.
Together we forge paths anew,
In the gentle tug, it's me and you.

Interwoven Paths

Two lives dance in a tender weave,
Each thread a story we believe.
Through valleys deep and mountains high,
Interwoven paths under the sky.

With every shared word and fleeting glance,
Two souls entwine, a cosmic dance.
In laughter, tears, we find our way,
Interwoven dreams that softly sway.

Through seasons change and moments fleet,
Your heartbeat echoes, a steady beat.
In the tapestry of hopes and fears,
We stitch our memories through the years.

Though paths may twist and sometimes stray,
The bonds we share will guide our way.
Together we'll face what comes to be,
In this interwoven harmony.

So here's to journeys, both near and far,
With you beside me, my guiding star.
In every turn, we find our truth,
In interwoven love, eternal youth.

The Strength of Shared Sorrow

In shadows deep where silence reigns,
Shared sorrow courses through our veins.
A heavy heart, a fragile thread,
Yet strength emerges where we tread.

When burdens weigh, and tears do fall,
We lean on each other, through it all.
In whispered words, we find release,
In shared sorrow, we find peace.

Though darkness looms and spirits tire,
Together we fan the flickered fire.
In every struggle, hands intertwined,
The strength of hearts, so well-defined.

For in the depths, we learn to stand,
With every tear, a stronger hand.
In the echo of struggles shared,
Resilience blooms, a bond declared.

So let us walk this winding road,
Through shared sorrow, we will erode.
Together we rise, we face the night,
In strength united, we find our light.

Salutations of Support

In the shadow, you may stand,
A gentle hand, a silent band,
Together we will rise and cope,
With every word, we weave our hope.

When storms arise, we're side by side,
In every fear, we will abide,
A comforting word, a tender gaze,
Through darkest nights, we'll find our ways.

Let laughter echo, let worries fade,
In every heart, the love is laid,
With open arms, we greet the day,
In each embrace, we find our way.

With spirits bright, we lightweight tread,
On paths of grace where fears are shed,
With shoulders strong, we stand as one,
Together shining like the sun.

So speak your truth, let your heart sing,
In unity, we find our wings,
With every trial, we'll stand tall,
In the tapestry of love, we'll crawl.

Graced Connections

A glance of kindness, a knowing smile,
In fleeting moments, we reconcile,
Every heartbeat a song of fate,
In quiet realms, we cultivate.

With threads of laughter interlaced,
We navigate this wondrous space,
In shared stories, our hearts align,
In graced connections, love will shine.

Through whispered dreams and hopeful pleas,
Our spirits dance like rustling leaves,
In gentle winds, we find our way,
With every word, we light the day.

Together we wander, hand in hand,
Creating memories, a sacred strand,
In every heartbeat, a bridge we make,
United in love, for each other's sake.

With every encounter, we grow anew,
In this vast world, it's me and you,
With open hearts, our souls explore,
In graced connections, we long for more.

The Safety of Kindred Refuge

In the heart of solace, we find our peace,
A refuge woven, where troubles cease,
In shadows dim, our spirits lift,
In each embrace, we discover gifts.

With whispers soft, our secrets shared,
In sturdy bonds, we show we cared,
Through trials faced, our courage glows,
In kindred refuge, love always flows.

With every tear, a flower blooms,
Our laughter chases away the glooms,
In gentle warmth, we all belong,
In unity's arms, we grow strong.

Step by step, in trust, we tread,
In heartfelt spaces, worries shed,
With every moment, our spirits thrive,
In the safety of refuge, we revive.

So find your place, we'll hold you near,
In this warm circle, free from fear,
With open hearts, we build our home,
In kindred refuge, we're never alone.

The Symphony of Solace

In quiet hours, a gentle song,
A symphony where souls belong,
With every note, a heart beats free,
In melodies, we learn to see.

Through trials faced, we find the tune,
In twilight whispers, beneath the moon,
Each harmony, a story told,
In the symphony, our dreams unfold.

Like rivers flowing, we intertwine,
In every measure, a love divine,
With laughter bright, our spirits sway,
In the music, we share our day.

Together we rise on wings of grace,
In every echo, a warm embrace,
With every heartbeat, a steadfast beat,
In symphonies, our souls will meet.

So lift your voice, let the music soar,
In this grand symphony, we want more,
With open hearts, we play our part,
In the symphony of solace, we'll start.

Nestled in Comfort

In the cozy nook, I find my space,
Wrapped in warmth, a soft embrace.
Whispers of peace in the air stay,
Guiding my thoughts, showing the way.

Outside the world spins fast and bright,
But here in my nest, I take to flight.
Dreams come gently, like leaves in the breeze,
Cradled in comfort, my heart finds ease.

A cup of tea with a tender sigh,
The flicker of candlelight, oh so spry.
Pages of stories, time drifts away,
Nestled in comfort, I gladly sway.

The shadows lengthen, the stars awake,
In this small haven, no heart can break.
Moments of stillness, gentle and true,
Nestled in comfort, I find my hue.

With every heartbeat, I feel alive,
In this sacred space, my soul can thrive.
Here's to the joy that softly stings,
Nestled in comfort, my spirit sings.

In the Heart's Sanctuary

In the heart's sanctuary, whispers dwell,
Where secrets of silence weave their spell.
Gentle echoes of love and grace,
A refuge of light in a crowded space.

The walls are adorned with laughter's delight,
Moments embraced, both tender and bright.
Here lies a canvas of dreams and hopes,
Crafting the path where the spirit copes.

Each breath a prayer, a melody sweet,
In this sacred chamber, two souls can meet.
Harmony lingers, like notes in the air,
In the heart's sanctuary, love is laid bare.

As the seasons change in the world outside,
In this quiet space, I can confide.
Wrapped in warmth, the heart beats bold,
In the heart's sanctuary, life unfolds.

Beneath a blanket of starlit skies,
I dream of the future, of love that flies.
In the quiet corners, peace takes flight,
In the heart's sanctuary, all feels right.

The Light That Endures

In the quiet dawn, light breaks,
A gentle touch, the world awakes.
Each ray a promise, soft and bright,
Guiding hearts through the night.

Time may pass, shadows may fall,
Yet in our spirits, the light stands tall.
It flickers, glows, a constant flame,
In every heart, it whispers your name.

Amidst the storms, when hope seems dim,
The light remains, never grim.
A beacon of love, a tender grace,
Forever shining in every place.

Through trials faced and paths unknown,
This light, our anchor, we've always shown.
In laughter shared and tears we shed,
The light endures, love's thread.

With every dawn, our spirits rise,
In unity, where our strength lies.
Holding fast, we'll not despair,
For the light that endures is always there.

Sharing the Weight

In life's journey, we all stride,
Together, side by side.
The burdens grow, but so do we,
Finding strength in unity.

Each step a story, a shared tale,
With open hearts, we will prevail.
When shadows loom and roads seem long,
In each other's arms, we grow strong.

Hands held tight, a bond we weave,
Through whispered fears, we believe.
Every struggle carried with grace,
Sharing the weight, we find our place.

In laughter's echo and friendship's glow,
Through thick and thin, we boldly go.
A tapestry formed with threads of love,
Guided gently from above.

Together we rise, together we fall,
In the dance of life, we have it all.
With every burden, a chance to grow,
Sharing the weight, our spirits flow.

Threads of Connection

Woven paths in the fabric of time,
A tapestry rich, a rhythm, a rhyme.
Through laughter and tears, we find our way,
Threads of connection guide us each day.

In the moments shared, we build a bridge,
Crossing chasms, we never hedge.
Every glance, a spark ignites,
In the dark, our love invites.

With every story, a layer unfolds,
Secrets whispered, tales retold.
In every handclasp, warmth is found,
Threads of connection forever abound.

Through distance felt and silence shared,
In the heart's echo, we are bared.
The pull of love, a steady force,
A guiding light on the chosen course.

Together we weave, together we spin,
In this dance of life, we both win.
Forever entwined, we'll always be,
Threads of connection, you and me.

Whispered Embraces

In the still of night, whispers blend,
Soft as shadows, they gently extend.
Each embrace a promise, tender and true,
In whispered moments, I find you.

Through the chaos, a quiet call,
In the silence, we rise, we fall.
A hidden language, soft and sweet,
In each embrace, our hearts meet.

Waves of comfort in the dark,
Every gesture leaves a mark.
In subtle sighs, our souls converse,
Whispered embraces, a gentle verse.

Held in this moment, time stands still,
A quiet promise, an unbroken will.
With every hug, a world created,
In whispered embraces, love celebrated.

Together we linger, without a word,
In our silence, a song unheard.
Wrapped in warmth, cherished and free,
Whispered embraces, you and me.

Symphony of Togetherness

In the gentle breeze we sway,
Notes of laughter fill the day.
Hearts entwined, we move as one,
Underneath the setting sun.

Voices harmonize in song,
Binding us where we belong.
Through the storms and through the strife,
Together we embrace this life.

Colors blend, our spirits soar,
Unified, we seek for more.
Hand in hand, we'll take this chance,
In this lovely, shared dance.

Dreams like stars, they light the sky,
With each moment passing by.
A symphony of hearts that beat,
Creating magic in the heat.

In this world, so vast and wide,
Together we can turn the tide.
With every note, our love grows strong,
In this symphony, we belong.

The Art of Forgiveness

In quiet moments, hearts can mend,
A simple word, a gesture, friend.
Bridges built from ashes, pain,
In understanding, love can reign.

Letting go of grudges held,
Releasing chains where once we dwelled.
With gentle whispers, wounds can heal,
Creating space to truly feel.

Through the cracks, the light breaks in,
A chance for new, a noble win.
Acceptance blooms like flowers fair,
In forgiveness, life is rare.

Words unspoken need to flow,
In the warmth of hearts that know.
Together, we can pave the way,
Embracing joy in every day.

A canvas fresh, we paint anew,
With every stroke, our bond rings true.
In the art of love, we find release,
In forgiveness, we find peace.

Hands That Patch

Hands that stitch with care and grace,
Mending hearts, in every space.
With each thread, a story sewn,
In the warmth of love, we've grown.

Fingers dance, creating art,
Binding pieces, heart to heart.
Through the fabric of our days,
A tapestry in countless ways.

With needle sharp, and kindness strong,
We weave together, righting wrong.
Hands that patch what life may tear,
Holding closely, showing we care.

Through storms and trials, we won't part,
Stitched together, never dart.
In every tear, a chance to mend,
With hands that love, our hearts ascend.

A quilt of memories, richly bright,
Together we will face the night.
As hands that patch, we'll stand and stay,
Bound in love, come what may.

Rekindling Flame

In the depths of twilight's glow,
A flicker dances, soft and slow.
Memories of warmth ignite,
In the night, a shared delight.

Embers whisper tales of old,
Stories shared, and dreams retold.
With each breath, the fire moves,
In this warmth, our spirit grooves.

Hands outstretched to fan the spark,
Together we can light the dark.
Passion swells like ocean waves,
In unity, this love behaves.

Through the trials, we remain,
Rekindling every lost refrain.
In the quiet, flames arise,
A testament beneath the skies.

With each heartbeat, we revive,
In the glow, our souls that thrive.
Rekindling flame, a dance so bright,
Together, we embrace the night.

Gentle Touches

Soft whispers in the night,
A caress that feels so right.
Fingertips like feathers glide,
In your warmth, I will reside.

Every glance, a tender spark,
In the dusk, we leave our mark.
With each sigh, our hearts entwine,
Together, love's design will shine.

Moments wrapped in sweet embrace,
In your arms, I've found my place.
Silence speaks in loving tones,
Within our world, I feel at home.

Every laugh a precious sound,
In your joy, my soul is found.
Gentle touches, soft and kind,
In this love, our hearts aligned.

Through the day, we roam as one,
Beneath the weight of setting sun.
Hand in hand, we'll walk this lane,
Gentle touches ease the pain.

The Love's Refuge

In your eyes, I see the stars,
A sanctuary from life's scars.
With every heartbeat, we align,
In your love, my soul's divine.

Whispers soft like morning dew,
In your arms, the world is new.
Sheltering from stormy weather,
In your love, we are together.

The laughter shared, the tears we hide,
In this refuge, hope resides.
As seasons change, our love will grow,
A gentle fire with steady glow.

Through trials faced and journeys long,
In your heart, I know I belong.
A sacred space where dreams unfold,
In your love, I find my gold.

Here we build our sweet domain,
In love's refuge, we'll remain.
A fortress strong against the night,
In your embrace, I find the light.

Shards of Light Together

Amidst the dark, we find our way,
With shards of light to guide each day.
In laughter shared, and secrets told,
Our hearts ignite, in warmth unfold.

Every moment caught in time,
A symphony, a perfect rhyme.
Together we'll face every storm,
In each other, we are warm.

Through trials that may come our way,
Hand in hand, we shall not sway.
With every challenge, love will grow,
In these shards, our spirits glow.

Finding strength in one another,
In your heart, I see the lover.
Through every joy, through every strife,
Shards of light create our life.

Together, we will shine so bright,
Guiding each other through the night.
With every fiber of our souls,
In these shards, we find our goals.

Healing in the Quiet Moments

In stillness, where the heart can mend,
Soft whispers cradle, love will send.
Amidst the chaos, find the peace,
In quiet moments, worries cease.

A gentle touch, a knowing glance,
In silence, we embrace the chance.
Each heartbeat brings a soothing balm,
Together in this tranquil calm.

With every pause, new strength we find,
In healing breaths, our souls unwind.
As shadows fade, the light will bloom,
In quiet moments, love's perfume.

Holding close through trials we face,
In stillness, we create our space.
Healing whispers, like a song,
In these moments, we belong.

Every glance, a promise made,
In the quiet, love won't fade.
Together, strong and ever true,
Healing moments, me and you.

Whispers of Mending Hearts

In shadows deep where lovers part,
Whispers soft can heal the heart.
Gentle words like morning dew,
Breathe back life when hope seems few.

With every tear that finds its way,
A chance to grow, a new display.
Two souls entwined, they start anew,
Finding strength in love so true.

The night may linger, doubts may rise,
But light returns with dawn's surprise.
Rekindled flames, their warmth bestowed,
With every journey love has growed.

So listen close to what is said,
In tender tones, old wounds can shed.
For love's sweet whispers softly guide,
Through storms of doubt, love won't subside.

Together they will face each fear,
In mending hearts, their path is clear.
Embracing all the hopes they seek,
In every moment, love grows sleek.

Ties of Solace

In quiet nights when shadows fall,
The ties of solace softly call.
In every glance, a promise made,
A sanctuary where hearts won't fade.

In laughter shared, in silence held,
A bond unbroken, gently spelled.
With every hug, a sense of home,
In cherished ties, no need to roam.

Through trials faced, they'll never part,
For in each other, they find art.
A masterpiece of memories bright,
That weaves their souls both day and night.

The world may change, time may insist,
Yet in their hearts, love coexists.
These ties of solace, strong and true,
Are love's embrace, forever new.

When life is hard, and paths are rough,
The ties they share will be enough.
In unity, they dance as one,
Under the moon, till night is done.

Threads of Connection

In every thread, a story spun,
Connection blooms beneath the sun.
In laughter shared and tears embraced,
Life's tapestry is interlaced.

With woven dreams, they find their place,
In every touch, a warm embrace.
The threads of life entwined so tight,
Binding souls in shared delight.

Through struggles faced, the fabric wears,
Yet love's strong threads repair the tears.
Together they lift each other high,
As vibrant colors grace the sky.

In moments fleeting, bonds may grow,
With every glance, feelings flow.
Threads of connection, bold and bright,
Illuminate the path with light.

So take my hand, let's weave and spin,
A tale of us where dreams begin.
In every heartbeat, we reflect,
The threads of love that we protect.

Embrace of Renewal

In every dawn, a brand new start,
The embrace of renewal warms the heart.
With gentle whispers of the breeze,
A chance to bloom among the trees.

As petals fall and seasons change,
Life finds ways to rearrange.
Through trials faced, old wounds may heal,
In love's embrace, they find what's real.

With open arms, they greet the day,
Casting doubts and fears away.
In gratitude for moments shared,
The ties of love make them prepared.

Each step they take, a dance of grace,
An inner strength that time can't erase.
In every heartbeat, rhythms flow,
The embrace of renewal starts to grow.

So rise with hope, let laughter reign,
In every joy, forget the pain.
With hearts ablaze, they'll journey on,
In the embrace of love, they are reborn.

Stitching Solitude

In the quiet corners, shadows play,
Threads of thought weave night and day.
A tapestry of whispers, softly spun,
Alone yet together, one by one.

Beneath a moonlit veil, secrets held,
Embracing silence, where hearts have dwelled.
Each stitch a memory, fragile yet bold,
In the fabric of time, stories unfold.

Alone we wander, yet never stray,
In solitude's embrace, we find our way.
The seams of darkness, gently aligned,
In stitching solitude, a peace we find.

Threads of stillness, woven tight,
A heart's quiet echo, a guiding light.
Through layers of silence, we craft our art,
In the tapestry of life, we mend the heart.

As dawn breaks softly, shadows recede,
A symphony of voices, a chorus freed.
In every silence, we stitch our place,
Finding solace in this endless space.

Unity in the Silence

In stillness we gather, hands intertwined,
Silent vows whispered, hearts aligned.
A language unspoken, yet deeply felt,
In the unity of silence, our fears melt.

Eyes meet and linger, truth in their gaze,
In the quiet embrace, our spirits blaze.
Voices may falter, but souls will sing,
In the calm of the moment, hope takes wing.

Each heartbeat a rhythm, a soft refrain,
In the garden of silence, peace will gain.
Together we rise, beneath the same sky,
In the bond we share, our spirits fly.

A tapestry woven of breath and dream,
In silence, we flourish, together a team.
Echoes of laughter, whispers of care,
In unity found, we lay our hearts bare.

With each gentle pause, a message so clear,
In the stillness of knowing, we draw near.
Together in silence, our spirits entwine,
In the unity of love, our souls define.

Fathoms of Empathy

Diving deep into another's sea,
Fathoms of feelings, you and me.
Wave upon wave, emotions arise,
In the depths of empathy, wisdom lies.

A touch upon the surface, ripples spread,
Carving paths where words aren't said.
In shadows, we wander, hand in hand,
In mutual understanding, we learn to stand.

Currents of kindness, flowing wide,
In the ocean of life, we safely glide.
With every heartbeat, a bridge we build,
In fathoms of empathy, hearts fulfilled.

Through struggles and joys, we silently share,
A mirror reflecting, showing we care.
In the quietest depths, connection thrives,
In fathoms of empathy, compassion derives.

Underneath the surface, treasures await,
In the sea of emotions, we navigate.
Deep within silence, our spirits meld,
In the fathoms of empathy, love is upheld.

Resilient Ties

In the storm's embrace, we bend but don't break,
Resilient ties hold when our hearts ache.
Through trials and tempests, we won't let go,
In the strength of our bond, we continually grow.

A thread of support in the darkest of night,
We weave our narratives, shimmering bright.
Through laughter and tears, hand in hand,
On the canvas of life, together we stand.

When life throws shadows, we shine like the sun,
With resilient ties, we face what's begun.
In the heat of the moment, we find our way,
Together in strength, we welcome the day.

Each moment a knot, tightly embraced,
In the fabric of trust, our fears are erased.
Through every challenge, we rise above,
In resilient ties, we find our love.

With every heartbeat, our stories entwined,
In the tapestry of life, our spirits aligned.
Together we flourish, through thick and thin,
In resilient ties, we create from within.

The Language of Solace

In whispers soft, the heart confides,
Beneath the stars where silence hides.
With every sigh, a story we weave,
In this gentle night, we learn to believe.

Time drips slowly, like honeyed gold,
In moments shared, our truths unfold.
The weight of the world, we gently lift,
In the language of solace, we find our gift.

Through tangled paths, we walk as one,
With every dawn, a new day begun.
Words unspoken, yet clearly felt,
In the warmth of love, our hearts can melt.

The moonlight dances on tranquil seas,
Cradled in hope, we find our ease.
In every heartbeat, a promise rings,
In the solace of each other, our spirit clings.

So hold my hand, we'll face the light,
Together, we'll conquer the longest night.
In the language of solace, forever true,
In every moment, I find you.

Rewoven Dreams

In twilight's glow, we gather near,
With threads of hope, we banish fear.
Each dream a stitch, in tapestry grand,
Rewoven glories, by our own hand.

Frayed edges whisper tales untold,
Of battles fought and hearts turned bold.
Through tangled yarn, our laughter flows,
In the fabric of friendship, love grows.

A loom of stars, where wishes splay,
We craft new paths, come what may.
With every challenge, a pattern unfurls,
In the dance of fate, we change our worlds.

The colors blend, as sunset fades,
In the silence, our courage invades.
With threads entwined, our spirits soar,
In the quiet night, we dream even more.

So let us weave with threads of gold,
In every heartbeat, our stories told.
Together we stand, unbroken, it seems,
In the art of life, we've woven dreams.

Breaking Through Shadows

When darkness falls, and hope feels thin,
A spark ignites, the light within.
With every heart that dares to fight,
We break the chains, and claim our light.

Shadows linger, but cannot stay,
For courage breathes, to light the way.
Each step we take, a promise made,
In the brave sunlight, all fears will fade.

Through whispered doubts, we find our strength,
In unity, we stretch our length.
With voices raised, we pierce the night,
In breaking through, we find our might.

Beneath the weight, we lift each other,
For every sister, every brother.
Hand in hand, we face the storm,
Together we rise, in our true form.

So when the shadows seek to creep,
Remember the promises we keep.
In every heart, a flame that grows,
In breaking through, our courage shows.

Tides of Support

In every wave, a hand reached out,
A lifeline tossed amidst the doubt.
Together we'll weather, storm or shine,
In the tides of support, our love will align.

The oceans roar, yet we stand firm,
With every crest, our spirits affirm.
Through raging winds, we anchor deep,
In the bond we share, our hearts will leap.

As currents pull, we hold our ground,
In the strength of love, we're tightly bound.
Each gentle wave, a whispered care,
In the tides of support, we're always there.

With every ebb, there's flow anew,
In every heartbeat, a promise true.
We rise together, against the tide,
In the ocean of love, we shall abide.

So let the waters rise and fall,
For in each challenge, we hear love's call.
In the tide of support, forever we'll stay,
Guided by hope, come what may.

A Chorus of Support

In whispers soft, we gather round,
Voices lift, a hopeful sound.
Together we rise, hand in hand,
In the strength of unity, we stand.

Through stormy nights and sunlit days,
We share our burdens, we share our ways.
In laughter's echo and tears released,
A chorus of support, hearts at peace.

With every step, we feel the love,
A bond unbroken, like stars above.
In darkest hours, we light the way,
Together we brave, come what may.

Each word a comfort, each hug a shield,
In moments of weakness, our hearts are healed.
Together we hope, together we dream,
A tapestry woven, a vibrant seam.

Through trials faced and victories shared,
In every heartbeat, we know we cared.
With every note, our spirits lift,
In the chorus of support, love is our gift.

Seasons of Togetherness

In autumn's glow, we gather near,
With falling leaves, we shed our fear.
Hand in hand, we stroll the lane,
In seasons of love, we dance through rain.

Winter's chill wraps us tight,
In cozy corners, we share the light.
With every story, our hearts ignite,
In seasons of togetherness, love feels right.

Spring arrives, with blossoms bright,
We plant our dreams, reaching for height.
In laughter's bloom, our spirits play,
As seasons shift, we find our way.

Summer's warmth, a joyful embrace,
In golden sun, we cherish the space.
Through every season, we grow and mend,
In this journey of life, you're my friend.

Together we forge, through time and tide,
In every season, we take the ride.
With open hearts, we stand as one,
In seasons together, our love is spun.

Weaving Joy Amidst Pain

Through shadows deep, we search for light,
In midst of storm, we hold on tight.
A thread of joy, we weave with care,
Amidst the pain, our hearts lay bare.

In grief's embrace, we find our song,
A melody sweet, where we belong.
With every tear, a flower grows,
In the tapestry of life, love always shows.

Hand in hand, we face the night,
In darkness found, we craft our sight.
With whispers soft, we share our tales,
Weaving joy through sorrow's trails.

Each heartbeat counts, a precious thread,
In every moment, we forge ahead.
Through trials faced, our spirits rise,
In unity found, we touch the skies.

Amidst the storm, together we stand,
Weaving joy, a vibrant band.
With every stitch, our story flows,
In life's rich tapestry, love only grows.

The Power of a Shared Breath

In silent moments, two souls align,
A breath exchanged, a spark divine.
In rhythms deep, our hearts entwine,
The power of a shared breath, intertwined.

Through whispered thoughts and quiet dreams,
In every sigh, a love redeems.
With open hearts, we learn to see,
In every breath, you're part of me.

In laughter shared, and solace found,
The world is lighter, grace unbound.
With each inhale, we feel the space,
In this connection, we find our place.

Through fleeting time, we gather strength,
In shared breaths, we go to length.
With every exhale, our worries flee,
In the dance of life, you're always free.

Together we rise, in harmony's song,
The power of a breath, where we belong.
In unity's grace, we stand together,
In every heartbeat, now and forever.

Crescendos of Comfort

In whispers soft, the shadows sway,
A murmur stirs at close of day.
Embrace the night, let worries cease,
In gentle arms, we find our peace.

Like ripples dance upon a stream,
Our hearts unite in tender dream.
Each breath a note, a sweet refrain,
Together, let us bear the strain.

When storms arise and dark clouds form,
We seek the light, a calming warm.
In quiet moments, hope takes flight,
And fills our souls with pure delight.

In every tear, a story flows,
In every laugh, the comfort grows.
Through life's vast symphony and song,
Together, we will carry on.

So take my hand, and hold it tight,
In crescendos, we find our light.
With love as shelter, we will stand,
In harmony, we'll build our land.

Wells of Understanding

In silence deep, we find our way,
Through gaze and touch, what words can't say.
We share the burdens, lift the weight,
In wells of understanding, love's our fate.

With open hearts and minds so wide,
We listen close, there's naught to hide.
In tangled thoughts, we find the thread,
A tapestry where senses wed.

Like rivers flow, our stories merge,
In unity, our spirits surge.
For every wound, we weave a balm,
In shared embrace, we find our calm.

So let us sit, nor rush the hours,
In depth of truth, we find our powers.
In simple acts of trust, we stand,
In wells of understanding, hand in hand.

In every glance, a world we see,
In every touch, the heart sets free.
Together in this sacred space,
We cultivate a saving grace.

Through the Cracks, We Bloom

In fractured soil where shadows lie,
A seed of hope begins to try.
Through cracks that form, a blossom breaks,
Defying odds, it stirs and wakes.

With each new dawn, the light draws near,
A gentle push to face the fear.
Resilient roots in darkness thrive,
In struggle's thrall, we find we're alive.

The world may try to dim our glow,
But in our hearts, the courage flows.
Through storms and trials, we press on,
In every struggle, new dreams spawn.

So let us show with vibrant grace,
That beauty finds a way, a place.
Through every crack, the bright reveals,
A testament to all that heals.

In fragile moments, hope takes form,
In darkest nights, we rise, reborn.
Through the cracks, we find our bloom,
Emerging strong, dispelling gloom.

A Nest of Kindness

In tender arms, our spirits nest,
A sanctuary, love's request.
In every smile, a warmth we weave,
A bond so strong, we dare believe.

With gentle words, we heal the hearts,
In kindness' reign, a work of arts.
Each gesture pure, a light anew,
In every moment, hope shines through.

Through storms of life, we stand as one,
In unity, the dark is done.
With open hands and hearts so wide,
We share the joy, we share the ride.

In laughter bright, in sorrow's hue,
We find the strength to see it through.
In every hug, a promise made,
In kindness nurtured, fears will fade.

So let us build our nest so high,
In love's embrace, we'll learn to fly.
In kindness shared, our spirits roam,
Together, we will find our home.

Gentle Currents

Whispers of the flowing stream,
Softly dance in morning's gleam.
Carrying tales from far away,
Each ripple sings a new day's sway.

In shadows cast by ancient trees,
Nature breathes a tranquil ease.
Fish dart by in gleaming light,
While leaves flutter, taking flight.

Mountains watch with timeless grace,
Guarding this serene, sweet space.
A world where worries fade and cease,
In gentle currents, find our peace.

Sunset paints the skies ablaze,
Moments linger, lost in haze.
The promise of a night so still,
Guides our hearts with whispered will.

As stars emerge and darkness deepens,
Dreams arise, the spirit steepens.
In waters calm, our souls unwind,
In gentle currents, freedom bind.

Healing Through Stillness

In quiet spaces, silence speaks,
A gentle balm for weary peaks.
Close the eyes, let the mind be free,
In stillness, feel the energy.

Moments stretch like stretching vines,
Each heartbeat calms and realigns.
Nature's breath, a meditative song,
In tranquil depths, we all belong.

Finding solace in the hush,
Emotions settle, thoughts can rush.
Yet in that pause, a spark ignites,
Transforming darkness into lights.

Beneath the noise, a whisper grows,
Awakening where love bestows.
Each deep inhale a chance to heal,
Through gentle breaths, the heart can feel.

So sit awhile in calming grace,
Embrace the stillness, find your space.
In healing moments, embrace the calm,
Through stillness, we become the balm.

Pathways to Peace

Twisting trails through fields of gold,
Stories of the brave and bold.
Each step forward, a choice to make,
On paths where doubts and fears can break.

Sun-dappled woods, the heart's desire,
Whispers of trees, igniting fire.
With every breath, a deeper peace,
In nature's embrace, worries cease.

Streams that babble like kind friends,
Carry burdens towards their ends.
Each stone a marker, each turn a sign,
On pathways where our souls align.

As twilight falls and shadows blend,
We journey forth with a steady hand.
In the soft glow of evening light,
Pathways to peace lead through the night.

So walk these trails, where dreams take flight,
Find solace under stars so bright.
With open hearts, we tread with ease,
Discovering life's sweet pathways to peace.

Sheltering Arms

In the heart of night's embrace,
A haven found, a sacred space.
With arms that hold us, warm and tight,
Sheltering dreams until the light.

Beneath the stars, soft lullabies,
Whispered hopes in soothing sighs.
Through gentle winds, love's song will soar,
In sheltering arms forevermore.

Each heartbeat echoes trust's refrain,
Woven comfort in joy and pain.
A bond that weaves through time and tide,
In arms of love, we safely bide.

When storms arise and skies grow gray,
These arms will shield, come what may.
With every trial, we stand as one,
In sheltering arms, new days begun.

So take my hand, let worries cease,
Together find our sweet release.
In these arms, where love is strong,
We'll write our tale, our heart's sweet song.

Reverberations of Comfort

In the quiet of the night, we find,
Whispers of solace, gentle and kind.
Echoes of laughter, warmth that stay,
In the heart's embrace, they softly play.

With every sigh, a story grows,
Through shadows, light gently flows.
Memories cradle us, tender and true,
In the tapestry of life, me and you.

Stars above sing their sweet tune,
Kisses of moonlight, bright as June.
A haven of peace, where fears dissolve,
In the arms of love, we evolve.

Through storms we weather, hand in hand,
Together we rise, together we stand.
With every heartbeat, courage ignites,
Reverberations of comfort, soft lights.

In moments shared, our spirits lift,
The smallest joys, a precious gift.
Together, we dance through the ebb and flow,
In the garden of kindness, forever we grow.

Rising Together

Through the valleys, we walk side by side,
In every challenge, we take the ride.
Lifting each other, hand in hand,
Together we flourish, together we stand.

With hearts aligned, our dreams take flight,
In the dawn's embrace, we chase the light.
United in spirit, we break the chains,
In the dance of resilience, strength remains.

Every step forward, a story unfolds,
In the warmth of connection, every soul holds.
Building a future, bright and bold,
In the chapters of life, together we're told.

With open arms, we greet the dawn,
In the echoes of laughter, worries are gone.
Rising together, through sundry skies,
In the heart's rhythm, our hope never dies.

We gather the shards of yesterday,
Mending the cracks in a beautiful way.
With dreams intertwined, we paint the skies,
Rising together, forever we rise.

The Interlacing of Journeys

Paths weave together, like threads in a seam,
In the fabric of life, we share a dream.
With every step, a tale unfurls,
In the dance of time, our journey whirls.

Through the bends and the turns, we learn to see,
The beauty of fate, both you and me.
In the stories we share, our hearts align,
In moments of laughter, love's design.

Tangled in joy, with sorrows we meet,
Each heartbeat echoes, a rhythmic beat.
With kindness as our guiding thread,
In this vast tapestry, we forge ahead.

In the shadows, together we tread,
With courage as our compass, never misled.
From mountains high to valleys low,
The interlacing of journeys, together we grow.

Every twist in the path, a new delight,
In the glow of the stars, we find our light.
Hand in hand, we'll pave the way,
In the journey of life, we'll never stray.

Resonate with Healing

In the silence, whispers of grace,
Notes of compassion find their place.
With every tear, a river flows,
In the garden of healing, love grows.

Embracing the shadows, we learn to mend,
With open hearts, we begin to transcend.
Together we gather, the fragments of hope,
In the tapestry of life, we learn to cope.

Resonating with warmth, we find our strength,
In each shared moment, we go to great lengths.
As healing unfolds, we breathe in deep,
In the gentle embrace, our souls will leap.

Through the storms, we rise anew,
In the light of kindness, love breaks through.
With every heartbeat, we cherish the day,
Resonate with healing, come what may.

In the symphony of life, each note we play,
A melody of kindness guiding our way.
Together we flourish, with grace we ascend,
In the journey of healing, love knows no end.

The Covenant of Care

In whispers soft, a promise made,
To watch, to tend, never to fade.
Through shadows deep, in light we share,
Our hearts entwined, a sacred prayer.

With every trial, we rise to meet,
In gentle hands, our hopes complete.
We bind our spirits, strong and true,
In love's embrace, we find our cue.

The storms may howl, the night may call,
Together we stand, we shan't fall.
With each heartbeat, the vow we renew,
In this covenant, forever we grew.

Through laughter shared and tears alike,
With every moment, our souls we hike.
Together we shine, like stars in the night,
In endless dance, we take our flight.

So here we stand, in trust and care,
In every heartbeat, love we wear.
A bond unbroken, endlessly rare,
In this covenant, forever we bear.

Fragile Warriors

Upon the edge, we brave the fight,
With trembling hands, we seek the light.
Our hearts endure, though shadows creep,
In silence strong, our promises keep.

We wear our scars like badges bright,
In every struggle, we find our might.
Though fragile forms may bend and sway,
Our spirits rise and never fray.

Through tempest winds, we chart our course,
In unity, we find our force.
With every breath, resilience grows,
In tender hearts, true courage glows.

The battles fought, the scars we bear,
In whispers low, we find our prayer.
Together we stand, in strength we find,
Our fragile hearts, entwined and aligned.

So raise your voice, let it be heard,
In every moment, love's the word.
We're fragile warriors, proud and free,
In our shared journey, we learn to be.

With hope in hand, and stars in sight,
We forge ahead, in courage's light.
Each step we take, a tale retold,
As fragile warriors, brave and bold.

Synergy of the Soul

In quiet moments, we intertwine,
Two spirits blend, a dance divine.
With rhythm soft, our hearts conspire,
In this embrace, we lift each other higher.

From every word, to every glance,
We weave a tale, a vibrant dance.
In laughter shared, the echoes unfold,
A synergy, eternally bold.

Through trials faced, we stand as one,
In darkness deep, we find the sun.
Our souls align, in perfect flow,
In every heartbeat, love will grow.

With every breath, your presence near,
A bond unyielding, pure and dear.
In the tapestry of life's embrace,
The synergy we share, time cannot erase.

So hand in hand, we brave the tide,
In this journey, we shall abide.
Together we rise, through joy and strife,
In synergy, we find our life.

With hope as guide, and dreams unbound,
We sail the seas, where love is found.
In every heartbeat, harmony swells,
In synergy of the soul, our story dwells.

Unseen Threads

In the hush of night, connections weave,
Unseen threads, in hearts they cleave.
With every sigh, the silence hums,
A tapestry of love that comes.

Through paths we take, our souls align,
In whispered dreams, a bond divine.
Though miles apart, the threads remain,
In every joy, in every pain.

Invisible ties, so strong yet light,
They lead us back when lost from sight.
In every heartbeat, a call we hear,
In the unseen, we draw near.

With gentle hands, we weave our fates,
In life's embrace, love radiates.
Through trials faced, and joys we share,
These unseen threads, an everlasting care.

In every laugh, a sparkle shines,
In every tear, the love defines.
Though hidden, trust is what we find,
In unseen threads that tie mankind.

So as we journey, let hearts be free,
In the strength of love, we shall be.
With every step, these bonds we thread,
In unseen ties, our hearts are led.

Milton Keynes UK
Ingram Content Group UK Ltd.
UKHW021208261024
450281UK00007B/97